Mystic Saints of India : 10

Sri Aurobindo

B.K. Chaturvedi

Series Editor : (Dr.) Mahendra

Books For All
Delhi-110052

Distributed by
D. K. Publishers Distributors Pvt. Ltd.
24, Ansari Road, Darya Ganj,
New Delhi-110 002
Phs. : 327 8368, 326 1465, 327 8584
Fax : 326 4368
E-mail : dkpd@del3.vsnl.net.in
Web site:www.dkpd.com.

First Published : 2002

ISBN 81-7386-251-6 (Sri Aurobindo)
ISBN 81-7386-231-1 (Series)

Published by
Books For All
(an imprint of Low Price Publications)
A-6, Nimri Commercial Centre,
Near Ashok Vihar Phase-IV, Delhi-110 052
Ph. : 740 1672, 745 2453
E-mail : lpp@nde.vsnl.net.in
Web site:www.lppindia.com.

Printed at
D. K. Fine Art Press Pvt. Ltd.
Delhi-110052 Ph. 745 2451

Printed in India

Introduction

Inclusion of Sri Aurobindo in this series might raise a few eyebrows since there is hardly anything common between him and the famous mystic saints that have already figured in this series. Nevertheless, Sri Aurobindo is a famous saintly figure in his own right. His experiments and experiences in the yoga descriptions, his contribution in preparing his countrymen to mentally accept India's independence as their ultimate dream and his creative works like the epic 'Savitri' place him on a different pedestal of the saints and social reformers that India still desiderates for.

This book represents a humble attempt to reveal the multifaceted personality of this most modern Indian mystic saint. Although most of the material for this book has been borrowed from Sri Aurobindo's own works, an attempt has been made to interpret and assess the significance of the same, not only in his time and circumstances but their impact today as well. In developing his personality, copious quotations from his poems/articles and comments have been used as also his contemporaries' opinions about him. Since he mostly wrote in English, the quotations used in here have their authenticity beyond doubt, for mostly they come from Sri Aurobindo's own writing or the material made available by the Aurobindo Ashram in Pondicherry. It is hoped that our readers would also find it worthy of inclusions in their personal library as they found the other books of this series. Lastly, the author shares with his readers the gratitude he feels for Pradeep Mittal of "Books for All" for giving him a free hand in the writing of this book.

B.K. Chaturvedi

SERIES' EDITOR'S NOTE

In 1963, Dr. Radhakrishnan, the President of India, declared in Bombay, "The time has come for all countries to work towards making the world a single home for Humanity.....Economics, Politics and transport have done their jobs. But we have to do as to give a soul to the world which has found a body, you can give it if you are truly Indian." We Indians are proud to have so many mystic saints who contributed to the upliftment of humanity.

In Indian thought, there are two modes in which we acquire knowledge: Argument and Experiment. Both these modes, together with experience play an important role in the development of mankind. Saints of India, through their arguments, tried to communicate their experiences to human beings. This represents an adventure in thinking.

This series, it is hoped, will enable the reader, eastern or western, to understand and appreciate currents of Indian thought by depicting the life and writings of different saints. We have tried to portray the true picture of Indian culture. I am really thankful to all those who have helped in preparing and publishing these books, as they will not only propagate the ideas of Indian saints, but also help in making mankind a better race.

Our world becomes wider, our imagination richer and our life more colourful and more zestful as a result of our companionship with these saints, who are the travellers of the spirit and the pioneers of thought.

25.7.01 **(Dr.) Mahendra**

5

Back Home

It was in February 1893 that his ship Carthage anchored in Bombay harbour. His turmoiled soul received a kind of strange peace as he descended on the purifying Indian soil. A deep peace summoned him as he first stepped on Apollo Bunder which remained with him for many months afterwards.

Normally a young man returning from his long journey in a foreign country feels drawn to passing some time in leisure with his family. But first of all, much of this attraction Aurobindo had lost owing to his father's death. Now he was determined to be more responsible and mature. Pleasure, ease and leisure, he thought he could not afford any more. So he joined the service of the Gaekwad immediately and on Feb. 8, 1893 he joined his duty.

Meanwhile Sayaji Rao, who had secured a "Civilian" for Rs. 200 a month, gave him a lot of departments to control. He started looking after the Land Settlement Department, Stamps Office, Central Revenue Office, The Secretariat,

The Vahivatdar's Office. Then he became (informally at first) Professor of French at Baroda College, and later, also Professor of English and finally the Vice Principal of the college.

And at the same time, along with his usual work, the Maharaja used to call him to write important letters and drafts that needed careful wording, to prepare his public speeches for him or draw up documents and several other jobs of literary or educational type.

Although he was not his Private Secretary he used to do much personal work for him officially—without any complaint, with great diligence, and great devotion. It was Aurobindo's very nature to do his work with concentration, with love and joy, bringing it to its perfection. Despite his discharging these duties he neither ever flattered the Maharaja nor ever feared him. One of his colleagues at Baroda was to write later on: "Sri Aurobindo and I often used to meet Siyaji Rao. Often he would write the speeches for the Maharaja. "Once the Maharaja had to speak at a social conference. Sri Aurobindo prepared the speech and we three read it together. Then the Maharaja said: "Aurobindo babu! Could you not make the speech a little simpler? It is so good that nobody will believe it is mine!"

Sri Aurobindo answered: "Why unnecessarily change it? Do you suppose, Sahib, that if it is a little simpler people will take it as yours? Whether it is good or bad, they will say that the Maharaja always has his speeches written out for him. The main thing is to see whether the thoughts there are yours or not?"

Further ahead the same person writes: "He (Sri Aurobindo) spoke very little. When asked a question he usually used to say just 'No' or 'Yes' and stop - would speak no further. There was something Yogic about him."

Joining the National Struggle for freedom

Even before he completed his stay in India for first six months, with his keen eye sight he had realised the conditions of the country and the political movement slowly gathering momentum for its freedom.

It was about that time Aurobindo met his old Cambridge friend, K.G. Deshpande who had also been the member of the renowned 'Majlis' society. At that time he was editing a paper named "Indu Prakash". He remembered Sri Aurobindo's fiery speeches replete with powerful revolutionary thoughts oozing patriotism and his love for the motherland. Deshpande requested him to write a series of articles for his paper about the Indian National Congress of those days, its leaders, aims and objectives. Aurobindo felt this was the right opportunity to reveal his inner thoughts, so he agreed. Then began the series of articles under the suggestive title: "New Lamps for Old". Full of keen observation of the political situation he criticized strongly the prevailing moderate policy of the Congress in these articles and gave his thought to awaken the nation to the need of the times to prepare it for the future. He wrote these articles under a pseudonym since he couldn't have given his name while under the service of the State of Baroda. One of the conditions of the service was not to comment upon the political situation prevailing in the country:

His articles created a sensation even when only first two articles were published. The political circles were bewildered and the Congress started wondering as to who could be the writer of these articles? Although an enquiry was instituted to have the name of the writer revealed, it drew blank. Meanwhile, Ranade, the famous Maratha leader warned the proprietor of the paper that he could be charged with sedition on account of those articles and might be prosecuted as well. Some of the chief points made in the article are quoted below:

(a) "I say of the Congress, then, this — that its aims are mistaken, that the spirit in which it proceeds towards their accomplishments is not the spirit of sincerity and whole heartedness — the methods — are not the right methods— the leaders — are not right sort of men to be leaders — we are at present the blind led, if not by the blind, at any rate by the one eyed."

(b) "— by reflection or instinct to get a clear insight into our position and by dexterity to make most of it, that is the whole secret of politics, and that is just what we have failed to do."

(c) "We lose in sincerity which is another name for strength."

People were surprised as to whose pen was pouring out this series marked with subtle power of thought, a comprehensive outlook of the prevailing political situation in the country, in a language that at once lucid and soul-stirring, bubbling with patriotism and absolute selflessness.

But all that he wrote appeared to ring a danger bell in the mind of the proprietor of the paper who, then, asked him to write in a modified tone. Though he initially resented, later on agreed to write on the philosophy of politics instead of the practical side of politics. But he couldn't continue in this vein and soon lost interest. Nevertheless, his articles showed what the country needed at that time and thus awakened the people's consciousness about the shortcomings the country had and how to get rid of them. It is still amazing that a mere 21 year old youth could write all that. His articles did stir the political bigots of the nation but before they could identify him he lost interest in that series due to the constraints placed upon him.

Now the year was drawing to a close and Aurobindo thought of availing leave to visit his native place. He went to Bengal for the first time after his return from England and met his mother, his sister, his younger brother Basin and a host of other relatives. Sarojini, his sister recalled her impression of him: "He was still shy with a delicate face and long hair. He didn't appear to have undergone much change in outlook during his stay in London".

Enjoying his time with his family he left for Baroda after some days. He choose to go via Bombay where he met the great leader Ranade. Ranade was quite alarmed reading the 'Indu-Prakash' series of articles. He knew that Aurobindo had penned those articles. In half an hour interview he advised Aurobindo: "Instead of attacking and civilizing the Congress violently, it would be better to try something like jail reform. That work would be more useful."

Aurobindo was to reflect on this advice much later when he was kept imprisoned in Alipur Jail. He realized that this was the thought of the moderate leaders of that time. How could the 'Moderate even bear the fire oozed out by Aurobindo's thoughts?

As he returned to Baroda, he decided to devote more time in reading and studying and so he increasingly cut himself off from the Baroda state duties. His disillusionment with the Maharaja had commenced and so instead of doing anything else, he started to mentally prepare himself for his future activities. His first book of poetry: "SONGS TO MYRTILLA" was published. Then "Love And Death" was rapidly written and other verses on various thoughts. His famous poetry book "SAVITRI" had its first draft prepared during this period only. Apart from creative writing he also read, with redoubled gusto, Homer, Dante, Vyas, Kalidas, Bhavabhuti all by himself. Since he was working in Baroda state where most of the state work was accomplished in Gujarati and Marathi, he started learning these languages also. Bengali he had started to learn in England itself but now he called the well known author in Bengali, Dinendra Kumar Roy who helped him perfect his knowledge of the language and accustom him to converse easily in Bengali. Dinendra Kumar Roy lived with him for nearly two years as his companion. Roy assisted him also in getting the railway parcels book ordered by Aurobindo and they came thick and fast. They were in all the sophisticated languages of the era: English, French, German, Italian, Greek and Latin. But no sooner did they reach near him that Aurobindo would read them up. Even when he went on holidays, a trunkful of the books always accompanied him. It was a sort of mobile library which always accompanied him.

Dinendra Kumar Roy's first impression of Sri Aurobindo is quite interesting. He records it in the following way: "Before I met Aurobindo I had imagined him as a tall, stalwart figure, dressed from head to foot in immaculate European style, bespectacled with a stern piercing look and affected accent, quick-tempered and intolerant". But "frankly I was a little disappointed when I saw him! Here was a shy, dark youth, his gentle eyes filled with a dream, his long, soft, shining hair, parted in the middle and flowing down upto the neck; he was dressed in a thick coarse dhoti and close fitting Indian jacket and wore old fashioned slippers with upturned toes. Is it Sriyut Aurobindo Ghose?" I asked myself 'Is this the living image of the great scholar of Greek and French and Latin? Who could have imagined it, believed it?'

Mr. Roy further describes Aurobindo:

> "In the short time I lived with him I saw clearly that his heart was pure and unworldly. He smiled and laughed like a child, frankly and gently. The corners of his lips experienced a power of inflexible will, yet in his heart there was not a trace of worldly ambition or any human selfish motives. He had but one deep yearning rare even among the gods — to give his whole being as a sacrifice that humanity's sufferings may disappear— I used to stay with

him and as I gradually came to know him closely, I felt more and more that this man was not a man of this earth, he was a God come down from his heavens as though by some curse[1].

"He who would bring the heavens here
Must descend himself into clay
And the burden of earthly nature bear
and tread the dolorous way".

Continuing, Mr. Roy says: "—Always I saw that he lived like a real self-denying 'sannyasin' austere in self discipline but feeling deeply other's pain — He had but one aim in life, it seemed to me: to gather knowledge, and for its realization in the very midst of the world's noise and bustle he lived the hard life of a 'tapasvi' — I never saw him angry"

A Dignified Man

Of course Aurobindo was a man with a cool temperament yet at times he did show his temper if he found things going wrong. He would just not put up with them. Once the Maharaja issued a circular to the effect that all officers should go to work on Saturday and Sunday also. Although rest of the officers complied with it albeit most unwillingly, Aurobindo refused to work on these days. Even

---

1. In his poem 'A God's Labour' Sri Aurobindo gives the reason as to why the gods must come down to the earth:

though it could have been construed his defying the order of the Maharaja he couldn't care less. The Maharaja Sayaji Rao was furious when he heard about it and even resolved to fine Aurobindo heavily. When our hero heard about it he remained unmoved. "Let him fine me as much as he wants but I shall not work on these days." Subsequently Maharaja, perhaps realizing the illogicality involved and extortionist vein apparent in the order, himself dropped the idea. He must have realized that Aurobindo could not be made to submit before an illogical order. While writing about Aurobindo, Roy further says: "At times, in the evenings or late afternoon, a horseman would come from the palace with a message for Sri Aurobindo:

'The Maharaja will be pleased if you will dine with him tonight; or will you let the Maharaja know at what time it would be convenient for you to meet him?' Well, I saw that when he was short of time he would even refuse the invitation! Many people and personages longed for just one meeting with the Maharaja, spent months dancing attendance on him to obtain it, and here was a mere teacher who considered his own work more important that the Maharaja's favour!— "He [Aurobindo] was alone, he did not know what it was to run after pleasures, knew no luxury, so extravagance; he never spent even a pie in a wrong way, and yet, at the end of the month he had nothing left."

Money Matters

Sriyut Patekar, a Baroda Advocate reminisces about Sri. Aurobindo whom he knew very intimately. He writes:

"— I observed about him a total absence of love for money. He used to get a lump sum of three months pay in a bag which he emptied in a tray lying on the table. He never bothered to keep money in a safe-box under lock and key. Nor he kept any account of what he spent. One day I casually asked him as to why he was keeping money like that. He laughed and then replied: " Well, it is a proof that we are living in the midst of honest and good people'. 'But you never keep an account which may testify to this?'— Then with a serene face he said: "It is God who keeps the account for me. He gives me as much as I want and keeps the rest to himself. At any rate he does not keep me in want. Then why should I worry?" What a faithful surrender! Doesn't it convey his total devotion to His Schemes".

However, not withstanding his apparent carelessness about the money matters he used to send money regularly for the maintenance of his mother and Sarojini's education. Although his two elder brothers were also earning well, they gave no help to the family. When some of his relatives cribbed about his brother's stinginess, Aurobindo would defend them: "Dada (Benoy) is in Cooch Bihar State Service and so he has to maintain a certain high standard of living. Manmohan is married and marriage is an expensive luxury!"

His Power of Concentration

Charu Chandra Dutta, an old ICS and his friend and co-worker in the political field gives a remarkable instance to highlight his high power of concentration:

"Once, back from the College, Sri Aurobindo picked up a novel lying close by and began to read it while some of us were noisily engaged in a game of chess. After about half an hour he put down the book and took a cup of tea. We had often noticed him doing this sort of thing before and were eagerly awaiting an opportunity to test whether he read the book from cover to cover or only glanced through it. So, we at once subjected him to a 'viva' test. I opened the book at random and read out a line, asking Aurobindo to say what followed. He thought for a moment and then repeated the contents of the page without a mistake". No wonder he could read all books completely in no time. Such persons have a photographic memory. Their correlation between what the eye sees and what the mind reads and retains is amazing. It is believed that he could get as may as 15 to 20 books in one go which he would read and not casually glance through them in a week's time. His power of concentration and retention would have beaten a modern Computer hollow! His sharp memory, high power of concentration made him write 'gems' even when he was busy in his other secular and drudgery filled activities.

6

The Revolutionary Spark Gathers Flame

All this while the revolutionary spark in him was not dormant but continued to glow brighter and brighter. Sri Aurobindo had realized that any passive resistance to the British might not do the needful. Although he didn't see eye to eye with his moderate friends, he didn't oppose them either. He was quietly working toward the aim he had set his eye on for his motherland and for this reason, through the help of his friends had one Jatin Banerjee, a young Bengali, enlisted as a trooper in the Baroda Army to get military training for the revolutionary work. It was as a UP man that had been enlisted, for the British government had prohibited the enlistment of any Bengali in any army. After a year's training Sri Aurobindo sent him to Calcutta with a program of preparation and action to get men, means, money, materials for revolutionary activities.

That man proved to be extremely energetic and capable, formed a first group which grew rapidly, and entered into relations with other revolutionaries already working clandestinely in Bengal.

Another Spiritual Experience

When he was in Baroda in the very first year of his joining the state service he had yet another spiritual experience more profound than the one he had earlier. He was in the danger of a carriage accident when he had the vision of the Godhead surging up from within, who was the master of the situation and averted the danger. This was before he knew anything about Yoga or had any sadhana —just like the experience of the vast calm at Apollo Bunder, for his spiritual experience. Later on, he was to describe this incident in a very powerful sonnet entitled 'Godhead' whose few lines are quoted below:

"Above my head a mighty head was seen

A face with the calm of immortality—

His hair was mingled with the sun and breeze,

The world was in His heart and He was I;

I housed in me the Everlasting peace,

The strength of one whose substance cannot die."

Marriage And Intensification in the Revolutionary Activities

Year 1901 was a very significant year in Sri Aurobindo's life. Apart from his revolutionary activities which he conducted clandestinely, he was also aged enough, rather over-age by the norms of that era, to get married. He was twenty nine then. The marriage was arranged by a common friend and celebrated according to Hindu ritual.

His wife was his literally better half (!) for she was only 14 when her marriage with Aurobindo was solemnized. But before marriage an unexpected problem arose. As the groom had been to England the orthodox raised the question of purification rites. However, proving stronger in will than his father Aurobindo flatly refused any expiation as he had done nothing to defile his purity. Then the priests, in a reconciliatory view agreed that should he get his head shaved off, they would accept him as pure. But Aurobindo didn't accede to even this proposal. At last —as he describes in his words the happening "an obliging Brahman priest satisfied all the requirement of the Shastras for a monetary consideration!"

He describes his mood those days well in his "Letters to Mrinalini" which though were meant to be absolutely private, became public when the police searched his private papers when he was in the jail, and they were even produced in the court as evidence of the "brewing treason" in his mind. We shall revert to them a bit later.

Revolutionary Activities

During his vacation in the year 1902, as was his routine, he went to Bengal. There he practised rifle shooting and resolved with his other friends to form revolutionary centres in Bengal. He had not only joined the active revolutionary groups but even tried to bring the existing ones together. With a sword and Gita in his hands he gave the following solemn oath:

"To secure the freedom of India at any cost and not to declare the secret of the Society to anyone."

Other revolutionary societies had also been formed in Maharashtra and he had already become a member of the Bombay branch. About this time he sent his brother Basin to help Jatin Banerji in Calcutta. It was this Jatin Banerji who was given military training at Baroda. While Jatin used to work among the educated classes, Basin with another friend, Abinash, worked among the students. They organized these young men and under the cover of sports and games for lathi-wielding, fencing and even riding. This way they prepared the youth for revolution. Their work spread clandestinely but rapidly and soon they had tens of thousands of young men, charged with the spirit of revolution, under their command. Sri Aurobindo looked after these preparations indirectly. In 1903 again he was in Bengal to organize the revolutionary forces but soon he was called back by the Maharaja who wanted him to accompany him in his trip to Kashmir.

It was in Kashmir that he had yet another spiritual experience which he said: "the realizations of the Vacant Infinite while walking on the ridge of the Takht-e-Suleiman." It is a small hill which now has the temple of the Adi Guru Shankaracharya. Though now called Shankaracharya hill, earlier it was known as Suleiman Hill. He describes this experience quite vividly in his sonnet 'Adwaita'.

It was these experiences that made Aurobindo come to spiritualism. In his earlier life he had no belief in supernatural things but many experiences gradually turned him to realize their truth.

He had a friend, a disciple of Swami Brahmananda of Chandod. First he got lessons from his friend in Pranayama- postures and exercises whose results he describes in the following manner.

> "My own experience is that the brain becomes full of light. When I was practising Pranayama I used to do it for·five to six hours a day—. The mind worked with great illumination and power. At that time I used to write poetry— usually I wrote— about two hundred lines a month. (But) After Pranayama I could see an electric energy all around the brain."

In fact his mental state during this period is revealed best by his letters to his wife Mrinalini. They were produced as an evidence against him in the law courts, Nevertheless, they contain the first statement of the burning aspiration of his soul; his thirst for God his intense yearning to see him, and his passionate love for his motherland. They are originally written in Bengali but given below is their translation to help the reader learn about his inner thoughts.

In his letter written on August 30, 1905, he says: "I have three madnesses:

"The first is that I firmly believe that whatever virtue, talent, learning and knowledge and wealth that God has given to me, all belong to Him, and that I am entitled to spend only as much as is needed for the maintenance of the family and on what is absolutely necessary; whatever remains should be returned to God" —

"The second folly (!) has recently taken hold of me. It is this: by whatever means I must see God face to face, get his direct realization. The religion of today consisus of repeating the name of God every now and again, and in praying to him in everybody's presence and in showing to people how religious one is. I do not want it. If God is there, then there must be a way of experiencing his existence, of realizing his presence. However, hard the path, I am resolved to follow it— I would like to take you also along that path— Anybody can reach perfection by following it. But it depends on one's choice to enter the path.

"The third folly is this: Others look upon their country as a mass of water, number of fields, plains, forests, mountains and rivers, and nothing more. I look upon her as my mother; I worship and adore her. What would a son do when he sees a demon sitting upon his mother's chest drinking her life blood? Would he sit down quietly to his meals and enjoy himself? Or would he rather run to see to his mother's rescue?.

"I know I have the strength to uplift this fallen race. It is not physical power— but the power of knowledge. The prowess of the Kshatriya is not only the force; there is the fire power of the Brahmin, the blazing power of spiritual knowledge. This is not a new feeling within me. I was born with it; it is in my very marrow. It is to accomplish this great mission that God has sent me to the earth—"

At the end of this letter Sri Aurobindo writes: "The whole country is at my doors, seeking for shelter and help— millions of my brethren of whom many are dying of starvation

— They must be helped." He carried "the sorrow of millions in his lonely breast" as he said later in one of his sonnets.

He ends the letter with a tender request: "This is a secret I wanted to tell you. Don't breathe a word of it to anybody."

Although these letters reveal what was going in the inner recess of the mind of Sri Aurobindo at that time, his wife, perhaps didn't understand all that was written in them, for she didn't follow him. She lived in Calcutta till her death in 1918. But she had become the follower of the Ram Krishna Mission having been initiated into it by no one else but the saintly wife of Sri Ramakrishna, Saradamani Devi and was very fortunate to have found so great a spiritual refuge.

7

Yogic Experience And Politics

That Aurobindo was being drawn slowly towards Yoga and spiritualism has already been hinted at. Guarded by his friends, Aurobindo had gone to meet, early next year, Yogi Brahmananda in the latter's Gangamath at Chandod. He felt there a unique experience. The Swami generally used to keep his eyes closed when people went to pay their obeisance to him. When they all went to bow before the Swami he kept his eyes closed. But as Aurobindo did obeisance to him, Brahmananda opened his beautiful eyes and looked full at him — as if he saw something extraordinary or as if he had recognized someone he was familiar with. Aurobindo also felt a strange sensation looking at the Swami's open eyes.

At Chandod only he also had a very illuminating experience. Sri Aurobindo went along with some friends to visit a temple of Kali on the bank of the Narmada. He just strolled there, for he had no attraction towards image worship and was against all such practices. But when he went into the shrine he found a living presence in the image.

All of a sudden, as if in a trice, he understood the truth behind image worship. In one of his letters he mentions about it "You stand before a temple of Kali beside a sacred river and see what? — a sculpture; a gracious peace of architecture; but in a moment mysteriously, unexpectedly there is, instead, a presence — a power, a face that looks into yours, an inner sight in you has regarded the World Mother!" About this experience Sri Aurobindo has also written a beautiful sonnet, "Stone Goddess" whose few stanzas are quoted below:

"In a town of Gods, housed in a little shrine,
From sculptured limbs the Goddess looked at me,
A living presence, deathless and divine,
A form that harboured all infinity—
Now veiled with mind she dwells and speaks no word
Hiding until our soul has seen, has heard
The secret of her strange embodiment".

It was about this time that one of his friends, seeing his natural spiritual bent asked him to learn Yoga as well. Replying to him, he said: "A Yoga which requires me to give up the world is not for me I have to liberate my country." He felt that, "a solitary salvation leaving the world to its fate" was not the right thing for him.

However, soon thereafter, something transpired which showed him that yoga gives power, and he wanted power to liberate his motherland. It so happened that Barin, his brother, had caught a violent and clinging hill-fever. Although he was being treated, the fever refused to go. Just then a Naga Sannyasi happened to come wondering by. He took a glass of water, cut it cross-wise with a knife while chanting a mantra and asked Barin to drink it. And almost in a moment Barin was cured of his fever. This way Aurobindo got a direct proof of the power of Yoga. “So when I turned to Yoga”, he said much later "and resolved to practice it" — He writes: “I did it in this spirit with this prayer:

"If thou art, then Thou knowest my heart—

Thou knowest that I do not ask for Mukti,

I do not ask for anything which others ask for

Whom I love—"

I ask only for strength to uplift this nation

I ask only to be allowed to work for This people

So, when he started Yoga there was no conflict in his mind. He embraced Yoga and politics with the singular aim: to uplift his nation. He finally resolved that “The Sanatan Dharma, this is nationalism.”

Partition of Bengal (1905)

Soon after happened the Partition of Bengal’ which was a major event in Aurobindo’s life. When the British government passed this black act a tremendous agitation rocked the entire country. Agitated public meetings took place everywhere to protest against this act leading to an outburst of a revolt. This was the agitation that acted as a catalyst to rouse the nation from the slumber. The cries of 'Swaraj' and 'Swadesh' began to be heard everywhere leading to the Nationalist movement for the liberation of the motherland. The movement was no more clandestine and people openly came out against the British Rule in India.

Aurobindo contributed his mite to this agitation by writing a small booklet called "Bhavanis Mandir'. It was circulated throughout the country. Patriots and lovers of the motherland, the booklet urged, must have spiritual strength. To prepare them, a plan was worked out in some details. The booklet said that "A temple has to be built and consecrated to the mother of strength, the mother of India. We will build it— in a high and pure air steeped in calm and energy." Here was to be "trained a new order of the Karma yogins", the men who had renounced all in order to work for the Motherland; for the freedom of the country.

The booklet urged the countrymen to come forward and sacrifice something for their motherland. It explained: "For what is our mother-country? It is not a piece of earth— It is mighty Shakti — The Shakti— we call India, Bhavani Bharati, the living unity of the Shaktis of three hundred million people— The energy of God is within us— It is to India that is reserved the highest and the most splendid destiny, the most essential to the future of the human race". It reminded all that "Spiritual energy is the source of all other strength— They are fathomless fountain, — heads, the deep and inexhaustible sources." It claimed "this infinite energy is the mother of Universe, the mother of worlds," Who says: "For you who are my children of the Sacred land,

Aryabhoomi, made of her clay and reared by her sons and winds—I am Bhavani Bharati, Mother of India." This small booklet exhorted all countrymen as none had done before; it was the call of the Motherland to all who were young and high spirited, to all her children to worship and serve her with knowledge in a complete self-giving, with strength gathered from spiritual living and enlightenment. Thousands of youths answered the call. This small book did what prolonged speeches of the top leader of that time couldn't achieve. It contained the 'Clarion Call' of the time which gave rise to such a national struggle which continued till the country achieved independence in the year 1947.

8

Plunge Into The National Struggle

As was his yearly routine, Aurobindo visited Bengal every year and during his holidays from the duties of the Baroda states. But this time he had gone their with a strong resolve, an unflinching determination to plunge deep into political activity. Now it was time Aurobindo couldn't have been away from his Karmabhoomi. So next year when the National College was started in Calcutta, he threw away the Baroda College job fetching him Rs. 710/- p.m. to join as the Principal of the new college in Calcutta for a comparatively paltry salary of Rs. 150/- per month. Now he wanted to serve the nation openly without any facade. He had no love for money and he never cared for it. It was a commitment of his inner conscience which he could not ignore any more. Fortunately, at that very time a Bengali paper, 'YUGANTAR' had started to preach open revolt and absolute defiance of British Rule. Sri Aurobindo wrote several opening articles in the early numbers of this paper whose editor was no one else but his own brother, Barin. The paper had as its chief writers three of the ablest young men in Bengal. Soon this paper earned a nook for itself in the intelligentia of the country. Specially when one of the sub-editors was prosecuted, and under Aurobindo's stern command the YUGANTAR refused to defend itself in a British Law Court, the paper gained all the more prestige and influence all over the country. Then something happened which made this Karma-Yogi take a head on collision with the British Empire.

The Editor of "BANDE MATARAM"

The editor of this paper was Bipin Chandra Pal. On his request through a common friend Aurobindo agreed to join this paper as one of the editors. He took this opportunity to start the public propaganda necessary for granting momentum to the revolutionary process. He started his job of awakening the country men by impressing upon them that complete and absolute independence was the aim of the political action in India. He used this journal to hammer this point repeatedly. He was the first Indian politician to have done this so openly. And he was a great success in his missions. It might not be known to many but the fact is that it was he who first circulated the term 'Swaraj' so extensively that still it is very much in currency. The journal declared and developed a new political program calling its phases the following way: non-cooperation, passive resistance, Swadeshi, boycott, national education, popular arbitration etc. Perhaps the greatest contribution of Sri Aurobindo to the national struggle was his coining very apt words which came very handy to the subsequent leaders including Gandhiji. He not only coined most of these words and hammered so deeply in the people psyche that they came to identify these terms with our country's national struggle. Aurobindo wanted to push the whole nation into an intense and organized political activity. His plan was to capture the Congress and make it an instrument of revolutionary action instead of a timid constitutional agitation which would only talk and pass tame resolutions. He also organized a central revolutionary body, an extremist party whose duties were listed as below:

(a) Increasing non-cooperation and passive resistance to make the foreign government's task difficult and increasingly tending towards impossibility.

(b) Creating a universal unrest to wear down repression:

(c) Finally, if need be, inciting a revolt all over the country.

The plan included boycott of British goods. creating national schools, arbitration courts of the people and the volunteer forces.

Sri Aurobindo wrote a series of articles on Passive Resistance, and another series developing a political philosophy of revolution. It was his intention to destroy all the wrong ideas created by the Moderate Party about British justice and benefits bestowed by a foreign government, their faith in British law courts and in the ruinous education that the British controlled colleges disseminated. On the contrary, he stressed that the stagnation or slow progress, the poverty, economic dependence crippled industries were all the evil results of a foreign government. He kept on hammering upon the countrymen's hearts that even though an alien rule be benevolent it was no substitute for a free and healthy nation.

His thought provoking articles, editorials etc. began to surge a new wave charged with patriotism and self respect. Soon the 'Bande Mataram' began to circulate throughout India. No earlier journal or paper had acquired such a reputation. It was unique in the influence it exercised in converting the mind of the people and preparing it for final revolution. However, despite all these incisive and at times 'inciting treason'- articles were so cleverly written that the police could not get enough evidence to prosecute Sri Aurobindo. This made a British editor even complain that though this paper reeked with sedition, oozing from its every line, yet was so cleverly worded that no legal action could be taken.

Through the medium of the 'Bande Mataram' Aurobindo created a new spirit in the country. Enthusiasm swept surging every where with the cries of "Bande Mataram' resounding the firmament. Suddenly the countrymen felt as though they were awaking to a new life in which it was glorious to be alive to act together with hope. The old apathy and timidity were broken and a force created which nothing could destroy. It rose again and again in the billowing waves bubbling with complete victory to India. He expressed this feeling thus:

"I saw the mornings of the future rise,

I heard the voices of an age unborn"

The country had experienced nothing of this kind ever earlier. Perhaps this was the time the foundation of the intellectual revolution was laid which, subsequently strengthened by Tilak, Gandhi, Nehru etc. saw the British march back to their island country.

However, as was his wont, Sri Aurobindo, preferred to remain and act, even to lead from behind the scenes. He says: "History seldom records the things that were decisive but took place behind the veil, it records the shown front of the curtain."

Nevertheless, he was thrust into the public view when the government prosecuted him as the editor of 'Bande Mataram'. However it couldn't find enough evidence to trap him in any legal case. But from that time he openly became the leader of the National Party. He organized the party's policy and strategy. Since, then he started leading the party from the front. He organized may political conferences, spoke on the public platform and addressed large public meetings all over the country.

Deeksha [Initiation] As The Revolutionary

It was this time that he thought of giving the 'Deeksha' (initiation) into the revolutionary way of life. What he said at that time in a private interview to Amarendranath Chatterjee, who became a well-known revolutionary leader later, is most touching. It was Mr. Chatterjee who received from him the Deeksha. He was told by Sri Aurobindo.

"If we want to secure the freedom of the country, we have to sacrifice everything for it— Is it so difficult to sacrifice oneself for the motherland?— If India does not become free, man also will not be free— Surrender yourself to God and in the name of the Divine Mother and get along with the service of India. This is my deeksha to you."

Amarendranath Chatterjee said later. "This deeksha moulded my whole life; all fear, all attachment left me."

And so, indeed, it was for him, in the midst of the most intense political activity, whilst he was writing fiery newspaper articles everyday; whilst he was speaking to enormous gatherings and rousing the whole country to cry of freedom, something from behind was urging and driving him deeper and deeper into the spiritual life. Now Aurobindo took to Yoga more seriously. For he had seen that it could give power, and he felt that with this power he could free India. Sri Aurobindo always said humorously: "Mine was a side-door entry into the spiritual life, but his mind was "upon great and distant things."

9

Nirvana (Renunciation)

Human mind is too intricate to be revealed no matter how closely one may watch one's activities. A man's outer activities one can describe but who can say with authority as to what goes within one's mind? Who can speak of the life of the spirit? Sri Aurobindo often said of his life: "It has not been on the surface for men to see." There is a famous Latin proverb which says: "Mentim homonis spectato non fruntum" [Judge the man from his mind and not from his appearance].

At this time Sri Aurobindo had come to a stage when he felt he wanted further guidance in his "sadhana". He spoke of this to Barin, his brother who knew of a Yogi, Vishnu Bhaskar Lele. Barin sent a telegram to Lele who, on receiving the telegram heard suddenly in a flash of institution: "Go to Baroda, you have to give initiation to a very great soul."

So, he came. Now, Lele wanted Sri Aurobindo to give up his political activities but this he refused. He agreed, however, to suspend them for some time. And he suddenly disappeared from the tumultuous political scene as quickly as he had entered into it.

For three days he stayed alone with Lele in a small room.

"Sit down", Lele told him, "look and you will see that your thoughts come into you from outside. Before they enter, fling them back."

Let us hear in Aurobindo's own words as to how he felt then:

"I had never heard before of thoughts coming visibly into the mind from outside, but I did not think either of questioning the truth or the possibility. I simply sat down and did it. In a moment my mind became silent as a windless air on a high mountain summit and then I saw one thought and then another coming in a concrete way from outside; I fling them away before they could enter— and in three days I was free— My mind became full of an eternal silence— it is still there."

As he further says, then followed there, "a series of tremendously powerful experiences— they made me see with a stupendous intensity the world as a cinematographic play of vacant forms in the impersonal universality of the Absolute Brahman— What it brought was an inexpressible peace, a stupendous silence, an infinity of release and freedom."

It was in this condition of these experience of the silent Brahman Consciousness that, a few days later, he went to Bombay. From the balcony of a friend's house he saw the myriad activities of the city, its whole busy movement as a picture in a cinema show, all unreal and shadowy. He describes this beautifully in his Sonnet, entitled 'Nirvana'

"The city, a shadow picture without tone,

Floats, quivers unreal; forms without relief

Flow, a cinema's vacant shapes— "

Eloquent Silence

He felt another, most moving experience around this time. While in that silent condition, he was invited by the Bombay National Union to address a meeting. Now, how he was to deliver a speech when his mind had become blank? But he couldn't refuse to speak either as he was a prominent and popular leader. But Lele told him to accept, saying, all would be well. This is how Aurobindo describes his that experience:

"I asked Lele: 'What should I do?' He asked me to pray. But I was so absorbed in the silent Brahman consciousness that I could not pray. So I said to him that I was not in a mood to pray. Then he replied that it did not matter. He and others would pray and I had simply to go to the meeting and made Namaskar to the audience as Narayana, and then some voice would speak. I did exactly as he told me— And all of a sudden something spoke."

It is claimed that it was a most stirring speech that he gave:

He exhorted all the audience as he never did: "Try to realize the strength within you, try to bring it forward, so that everything you do may be not your own doing but the doing of that truth within you— Because it is not you, it is something within you. What can all these tribunals, what can all the powers of the world do to that which is within you; that Immortal, that Unborn and Undying one, whom the sword cannot pierce, whom the fire cannot burn?—".

It was a time when he started feeling the Divine Guide within. This realization of the silent Brahman was so powerful that, as Aurobindo himself says, finally Lele "was made by a Voice within him to hand over to the Divine within me, enjoying an absolute surrender to his will—."

Lele also started feeling that time was gone when Aurobindo needed to be given any further instructions. Aurobindo also knew then that he could rely fully on the inner divine Guide within, he needed no human guru.

This absolute silence never left him. But how he was to accomplish the work left still unfinished? Sri Aurobindo answers: "I had the realization of Nirvana first , then came the experience of action: not my own but from above—"By this liberation one becomes free from ego, one becomes an instrument of the Divine Force— In the condition of absolute inner silence I carried on a daily newspaper and made a dozen speeches in the course of three or four days—."

This realization that he was only an instrument of the divine force made him return to full participation in political activity once again. For to him life became a field of the Divine. Now, he felt as if God was the leader of the political awakening. It was God who was working for the fulfillment of his own purpose. Sri Aurobindo felt that "something else than himself took up his dynamic activity and spoke and acted through him—." He gave many powerful speeches all the way down from Bombay to Calcutta, conducted many conferences in Bengal. Aurobindo felt as though his activities were being conducted by the Guide within himself. He adopted totally the path as the Gita explains: act as the divine instrument with neither any attachment to any action or dispassion to any inactivity. However, it was during this period that an event of great significance occurred. On April 30, 1908, at Muzaffarpur in Bihar, there was an attempt to throw a bomb at the district magistrate. Although Aurobindo had no hand in it, with several other revolutionaries he was also arrested on May 7, and his pilgrimage to prison began.

10

The Prison Pilgrimage

By this time a heady mix of spiritualism and revolutionary spirit had began to pervade the Indian society. Often the people started calling prison to be a holy spot, taking clue from Lord Krishna's birth in the prison from where he eventually liberated his parents. The popular feeling was that the motherland at that time stood imprisoned and going to prison was akin to going on a pilgrimage. This feeling was further strengthened enable by Sri Aurobindo's visit to Alipore Jail.

Early in the morning of May 2, while Aurobindo was still sleeping, the British Police charged up the stairs of his house with revolvers in their hands and arrested him. It was customary to arrest the freedom fighters during the wee hours in the morning since it helped the Police escape much public hullabaloo. Aurobindo was one of those young revolutionaries to be arrested then. In fact all over Bengal many revolutionaries on whom the Police had been keeping an eye, were arrested and jailed. Their houses were searched; and one of them, afraid that the party secret might leak out through him, shot himself. Even after the arrests the searches had continued.

Sri Aurobindo was taken to the police station and thence to the Alipore Jail. The famous trial began on May 19 and lasted nearly a full year. There were 42 accused, 4000 exhibits, about 300 to 400 other proofs and 222 witnesses. Aurobindo's sister, Sarojini, made an appeal "to the public spirit and generosity of my countrymen" for his brother's defence, and from every corner of the country, rich and poor sent their share of the support.

During his imprisonment Sri Aurobindo was first lodged in a solitary cell — nine feet by six , which served as bedroom, dining-room and toilet all in one — but was afterwards transferred to a huge room where he lived with other prisoners in the case.

However, after the assassination of the approver all the prisoners were confined in separate cells again, and met only in the court or at daily exercises where they couldn't talk.

Sri Aurobindo spent almost all his time in reading the Gita and the Upanishads as also in intensive meditation. He carried on his Yoga even when he had to live with others and associated himself to meditation amid general talk and laughter, the playing of games and much noise and disturbance.

Sri Aurobindo himself gives a glimpse to his prison life in the following words: "— I was taken — to Alipore and was placed in a solitary cell. There I waited day and might for the voice of God within me, to know what he had to say to me, to learn that I had to do — I remembered that a month or more before my arrest, a call had come to me to put aside all my activity, to go into reclusion and look into myself — I — could not accept the call. My work was very dear to me — He spoke to me again and said, 'The bonds you had not strength to break, I have broken for you— I had another thing for you to do and it is for that I have brought you here — to train you for my work."

While he was waiting he was in a great mental and physical distress. He further says: "I called upon God with eagerness and intensity and prayed to him to prevent my loss of intelligence. That very moment there spread over my being such a gentle and cooling breeze, the heated brain became relaxed, easy and supremely blissful, such as in all my life I had never known before. From that day all my troubles of prison life were over — that day in a single moment God had given my inner being such a strength that these sorrows — did not leave any trace or touch — it was possible to live happily during the long solitary confinement— I also realized the extraordinary power and efficacy of prayer." [This description is originally in Bengali and its translation has been used here]. He concludes his missive with this sentence: "A prayer — can link man's strength to a transcendent force."

It was in the Alipore Jail that he had yet another experience so marvellous that he describes it thus: [during the hours of walking] "I looked at the jail — and it was no longer by the high walls that I was imprisoned; no, it was

Vasudeva (Lord Krishna) who surrounded me. I walked under the branches of the tree in front of my cell but it was not the tree, I knew it was Vasudeva; it was Krishna whom I saw standing there and holding over me his shade. I looked at the bars of my cells, the very grating that did duty for a door and I again saw Vasudeva. It was Narayana (Lord Krishna or Vishnu) who was guarding and standing sentry over me— ."

"Or I lay on the coarse blankets that were given to me for a couch and felt the arms of Sri Krishna around me, the arms of my friend and Lover— . I looked at the prisoners in the jail: the thieves, the murderers, the swindlers, and as I looked at them I saw Vasudeva, it was Narayana whom I found in these darkened souls and misused bodies."

Even at the Sessions court everyday, in his iron cage his experience was no different. He writes further: "When the case opened — I was followed by the same insight — He said to me — 'Look at the Magistrate now — at the prosecuting counsel.' I looked and it was not the Magistrate whom I saw, it was Vasudeva, it was Narayana who was sitting there on the bench. I looked at the prosecuting counsel and it was not counsel — I saw it was Sri Krishna who sat there and smiled. 'Now do you fear?' He said; 'I am in all men and I overrule their actions and words.' Since he found no difference in whatever he saw whether in the prison or in the court, amidst the court proceedings, the whole day he remained absorbed in meditation, hardly attending to the trial and the evidence. He did not reply to the questions, he listened only to the voice within which repeated "I am guiding, therefore fear not. Turn to your own work for which I have brought you to jail."

He had even some supernatural experiences, that may be called quite bizarre and rather uncanny as well. For a fortnight he heard constantly the voice of Vivekananda, speaking to him in his meditation. It spoke on a special field of spiritual experience and then ceased.

Another remarkable experience was that of levitation. He was indeed concentration, and asking himself: "Are such 'siddhis' possible?" And suddenly he found himself raised up, half in mid-air, and the body remained suspended thus without any exertion on his part.

The jail warder had also seen this happen, and altogether dazzled, had spread the news everywhere. So much so, that at one time all over India people believed that Sri Aurobindo usually remained seated above ground!

—Concluding his experience, he writes: "Day after day he showed me his wonders, — things were opened to me which no material sciences could explain."

The Judgement Day

His case was defended by equally renowned personage, Chittaranjan Das. He was his friend. At first Aurobindo felt it would be necessary to give him instructions. But once again a voice within said: "This is the man who will save you— Put aside those papers. It is not you who will instruct him. I will instruct him."

After this experience he left everything in God's hands completely. On the last day of the trial, on May 9, 1909, whilst everyone in the court sat silent fearing the verdict of capital punishment — suddenly C.R.Das burst into such inspired speech that Judge, Jury and whole audiences were swept off in its surge of power:

[Some excerpts of that speech are quoted below]

> "—— Long after the controversy will be hushed in silence, long after the turmoil, the agitation will have ceased, long after he is dead and gone, he will be looked upon as the poet of patriotism, as the prophet of nationalism and the lover of humanity."

> "—— Long after he is dead and gone, his words will be echoed and re-echoed, not only in India but across distant seas and lands. Therefore, I say that the man in his position is not only standing before the bar at the court but before the bar of the High Court of History."

It appeared as the "Prophetic soul of the wide world dreaming on things to come" that spoke through his lips. Sri Aurobindo was acquitted for lack of evidence against him.

11

The Post—Prison Experience

Having stayed for about a year in the jail Aurobindo was released. It was his powerful Uttarpara speech in which he revealed his prison experiences that made him the object of people's great acclamation and renowned honour and love. From head to almost toe he was covered with garlands. Nearly to ten thousand men who heard his speech in pin-drop silence he was no less than an incarnation of God.

But as far as Aurobindo was concerned, all these experiences had brought about a deep change in his view of life: he had started yoga to get spiritual strength for his revolutionary work, but now the inner spiritual life and realization took him up entirely and his work became a part and result of this as also it now exceeded the service and liberation of India and fixed itself in an aim which was world-wide in its bearing. Now it concerned the whole future of humanity. For in the jail he had received the Divine Message:

"I am rising up this nation to send forth my word —
It is for the world and not for themselves that they rise —
I am giving them freedom for the service of the world."

Meanwhile, while Sri Aurobindo had been in jail, the political scene of the country had undergone a drastic change. Most of the Nationalist leaders were in the prison or in exile and hence the atmosphere was heavy with depression and discouragement. Yet the feeling of revolt, though considerably repressed, was silently growing stronger and deeper. In fact the more it was depressed the stronger it became.

Sri Aurobindo once again began his work, with greater determination to continue the struggle. He gave many speeches — the first of these being his famous Uttarapara speech. He attended many political conferences and started two weeklies: 'the KARMAYOGIN' in English and 'The DHARMA' in Bengali. The first carried the famous motto of the Gita: "Yogah Karmasu Kaushalam" (Yoga is skill in works). Soon these journals achieved a very wide circulation. Once again Sri Aurobindo proclaimed the ideal of absolute independence and advocated "no compromise", "no-cooperation". He would have nothing to do with the same reforms that the Government proposed: he declared them unreal and false and not acceptable.

But this was the period witnessing ruthless repression on the part of the government. Imprisonment's, arrests, accusations, deportations were the order of the day. Sri Aurobindo, however, chose to speak to the people directly, explaining them the true place of repression and its significance in the political movements. He said: "It is — a foolish idea — disproved over and over again in history, to think that a nation which has once risen, once has been called up by the voice of God to rise, will be stopped by mere physical repression— Repression is nothing but the hammer of God that is beating us into shape so that we may be moulded into a mighty nation and an instrument for His work in the world."

On its part, the Government was hell-bent to get rid of Sri Aurobindo again, and this time decided to deport him.

"I was informed," he commented humorously, "that I was qualifying for deportation." His fault being, as the Government perceived, his appearing to speak more than the Government could digest in his public meetings and wrote too much about freedom.' He was advised by his friends to leave British India and work from outside. But he did not agree with this idea. "It wasn't necessary!" He felt he could stop the Government's project by writing an article in the 'Karmayogin', 'An open Letter', about his threatened deportation, leaving to the country what he called, "My Last Will And Testament." This did serve his purpose for the Government had to give up the idea of deporting him. It had to wait for another excuse and it found an occasion when Sri Aurobindo wrote another signed article reviewing the political situation. One evening in February 1910, at the "Karmayogin" office he was warned of an approaching police search, and his arrest. Some of those present started preparing for the fight. Animated ideas were flying about when suddenly a distinct and a well known voice from above spoke three words:

"GO TO CHANDER NAGORE"! He obeyed the command at once, for now he acted as moved by the divine guidance. He did not consult anybody — not even his colleagues. Everything was done in the almost secrecy. It was about eight o'clock when he started and in ten minutes' time he was at the river 'ghat', having evaded the officially intelligent sleuths watching his office. An ordinary Ganga boat was hailed and he was on his way to Chander Nagore with his two youthful companions. Much later, expressing his feeling about this divine exhortation, Aurobindo was to say: "I would hear, in my spirit's wideness solitary.

The voice that speaks when normal lips are mute."

Many hear this voice but only few are able to catch it. Yoga practice had dissolved all the disturbance that stood between Sri Aurobindo's self consciousness and the divine Voice. Henceforth this was the sole guiding force of his life.

12

Stay In Chander Nagore And Escape To Pondicherry

It was yet dark when they reached Chander Nagore. Sri Aurobindo had reached there unannounced. Of course, his one friend, Motilal Roy knew about it and it was he who made secret arrangements for his stay there and looked after him.

Aurobindo says: "I came away because — I got a very distinct 'Ādesh'— I have cut my connections entirely with politics, but before I did so I knew from within that the work I had began there was destined to be carried forward — that the ultimate triumph of the movement I had initiated was sure — ."

Reaching there he plunged entirely into solitary mediation, ceasing all his political activity. Though he stayed in Chandernagore for nearly a month and a half the Government did not get the faintest scent of it. His visit was so secret and sudden that not even his co-workers knew where he had disappeared to. In Chander Nagore he was in total seclusion and absorbed in his sadhana. Motilal

Roy was to describe Sri Aurobindo's stay there in the following words: "— (he was) — A completely surrendered individual. One felt when he spoke as if somebody else were speaking through him — I placed the plate of food before him — he simply gazed at it, then ate a little; just mechanically! He appeared to be absorbed even when he was eating; he used to meditate with open eyes, and see subtle forms and spiritual visions."

Having stayed there for about a month, it was in the end of March that he received another command, this time to proceed to Pondicherry. It appears as if the inner voice had the fair idea of the geography as well as the administrative domination of the different parts of it! For it guided him to go from one French territory to another, safely avoiding any place under the British rule!

Getting this command Aurobindo asked Motilal Roy to make arrangements for his departure and wrote two letters: One to Amar Chatterjee at Uttarpara and other to his cousin, Sukumar Mitra at Calcutta. He asked both of them to meet at the river 'Ghat' and help him board the ship called "Duplex'. At the same time Aurobindo's young friend, Suresh Chakravarty - nick named Moni, received a note, telling him to go to Pondicherry and arrange for Aurobindo's stay there. Moni was also given a letter of introduction to one Srinivasachari, who was connected with the revolutionary Tamil weekly 'INDIA' which whole heartedly supported the nationalist policy. The famous Tamil poet and the one who raised the Clarion call in south for the independence of India, Subramaniam Bharati, was also working with that Srinivaschari. This paper with rebellious overtones used to get published from Pondicherry.

As the records and the letters written about Sri Aurobindo reveal, Moni, dressed as an Anglo-Indian to escape suspicion walked to the Howrah station and left by train on March 28. Sukumar Mitra was there to send him off after giving him an envelope containing Rupees thirty - a good amount then. Moni reached Pondicherry on 31st March. Reaching there he straightaway left to meet Srinivaschari with the introductory letter, asking him to arrange for Aurobindos' stay there, who was to reach there by April 4. But nobody believed Moni. On the contrary, they suspected him to be a spy. They felt that Sri Aurobindo would never choose to come to Pondicherry so far away from his place of action. Despite Moni's pleading with them to arrange a house for Aurobindo's stay they would not move. They delayed it so much that the day of arrival of Aurobindo also dawned. But no arrangement had been made till that day. Moni was very much troubled. He again told them:

"Sri Aurobindo is coming today and still you are doing nothing for his stay. After all, where will he stay?" Although they told Moni that the arrangement would be made when Aurobindo arrived secretly they thought to give Moni a sound beating when this news would be proved false. For till that time they were convinced that Aurobindo would never like to come to such a place so far away from his place of action. Despite Moni telling that it was Aurobindo's secret visit and he never wanted it to be publicized, they refused to believe him.

Meanwhile, on the other end, the things didn't turn out as planned. Sukumar Mitra, Aurobindo's cousin, who had received his letter in advance, was the editor of the journal called 'SANJIVANI'. Aurobindo formerly used to stay in Sukumar's house. With the result his house was constantly guarded by the C.I.D.

Getting the letter Sukumar made his plan. He prepared two trunks (for Aurobindo was to be accompanied by a friend call Bijoy Nag), called one of his Nationalist workers: Nagendra Kumar and Guha Roy, gave them those trunks and two real names taken from the SANJIVANI subscribers list and not the imaginary ones. Then he instructed them to buy two second class tickets for Colombo in order to dodge the police and the CID about the real destination: Pondicherry. Nagen bought the tickets and took the trunks with him. The next day, March 3, Sukumar asked them to hire a boat and take the trunks to the cabin of 'Duplex' ship. He was asked to wait with his boat for the two passengers who would come from the other side of the river and whom he had to take to the steamer. Seeing this elaborate and secretive preparation Nagen realized that one of the passenger was sure to be no one else but 'Aurobindo'. Sukumar eventually confirmed it but said that "keep it as a secret". He also warned him to be extremely cautious.

As previously arranged Amar Chatterjee met Aurobindo at the 'Ghat' and ferried him across to the Calcutta-side of the Ganges. But there was nobody to meet him!

At last he hired a coach and took Aurobindo to Sukumar's house, taking care, however to stop the carriage at a distance and inquire. But Sukumar was not at home. So they returned to the 'Ghat'.

Now, unfortunately, Nagen had been delayed in crossing the river and had missed Aurobindo's boat. He returned and informed Sukumar, who told him to go back immediately and retrieve the trunks from the cabin. It was already six o'clock in the evening when Nagen arrived. He found that the doctor who examined the passengers and issued health certificates had finished his work and gone home.

He took the Doctor's address from the Captain, got back the trunks and put them in the hired carriage. The coolie who carried the trunks, hoping to get a good 'bakshish', offered the information that he knew the Doctor's house and his servant too, and would manage everything. Nagen, much relieved, asked the coolie to wait there for him and drove back to Sukumar's. He found Sukumar anxiously awaiting him now; he asked Nagen to hurry back to the 'Ghat'; meet Aurobindo and arrange to get the Doctor's certificate. So once again he rushed and found Sri Aurobindo's carriage waiting by the way side. The coolie, too, was siting there, and quickly informed him, "Your Babu has come. I have told him about you. It is very late already. If we don't hurry the Doctor will go to sleep". Nagen then had the trunks shifted to Aurobindo's carriage and got in himself. The coolie climbed up to the coach-box and they drove to the doctor's house. Bijoy Nag sat besides Sri Aurobindo; he was to accompany him to Pondicherry. The coolie spoke to the Doctor's servant and the medical inspection was arranged. But they have to wait for half an hour before they were called in by the Doctor. There, on the verandah, while the young men talked all the time,

Aurobindo sat utterly silent. Strangely, the coolie, having noticed this, went and whispered to Nagen:

"Your Babu seems frightened. Perhaps he has never faced an English saheb and is afraid. Please tell him that the doctor is a good man there is no need to fear." Nagen replied: "No, Babu is not afraid; he was suffering from malarial fever and looks weak, so you may have thought he is frightened." But the coolie was not at all convinced! He ran to Aurobindo and said: Babuji, why are you so frightened? The doctor is a very good man you need not fear him." He even caught Aurobindo's arms and shook them a little. The young men looked at each other at this strange behaviour, and smiled. Sri Aurobindo also smiled softly. Within minutes the medical exam was over and the needed certificate obtained. But in that short time the Doctor remarked: "The passenger spoke English like an Englishman." Immediately they rushed to the 'Ghat'. As they went the young men still anxious and worried as to how all would go off. But pristine calm flitted across Aurobindo's face; there was no trace of any kind of anxiety and restlessness. He sat unmoved, quiet, almost like a statue - as if in deep meditation. Aurobindo knew that he who had destined his fate could never go wrong. It was nearly eleven o'clock when they reached the 'ghat' and Sri Aurobindo and Bijoy Nag boarded the steamer 'Duplex'. Nagen duly touched his 'Aurobindo's feet and returned with a heavy heart. He knew that he might not see him now. It was in the early hours of the next morning, on April 1, 1910, the steamer left Calcutta. The police and the CID had no idea where their 'culprit' might have escaped to.

13

Pondicherry The Base Permanent

When at 4 p.m. on April 4, 1910, the 'Duplex' touched Pondicherry, Srinivaschari and Moni were at the port to welcome Sri Aurobindo. They immediately took him to Shankar Chetty's house, the same house in which Swami Vivekananda had also stayed during his tour of South India, as his guest. About a week after it was at this house that someone came to meet Aurobindo for a very special and important reason. He wanted to meet a Yogi for "he had been sent from France by Mira" [Who was subsequently called mother] with a special mission. She had sent a sketch of a 'Yoga chakra' (a mystic symbol), saying that its interpreter would be found in India. It was also conveyed that "he would be the master and guide in Yoga." Sri Aurobindo gave the required interpretation to that symbol.

It might appear bizarre in the present context but the fact was that Mother, who was then practising her own yoga in France, since a very long time, had developed an inner contact and a kind of communion with Sri Aurobindo. Only outwardly they were still strangers to each other. There was yet another person who knew thus inwardly about Aurobindo and who was the famous Yogi Nagai Japata, who lived near Trichirapalli. When on his deathbed he called his disciples around him, one of them, a rich Zamindar, K.V.R. Iyengar. This man asked his master to whom he should go for spiritual guidance in future. Nagai Japata remained silent for a while, then said that a 'Mahayogi' would come from the North- "Uttaryogi"- whose help he could take. But as many yogis were rather peripatetic by nature and constantly moved from North to South, the disciple asked as to how would he be able to recognize that particular one. Then, it is said, Nagai Japata, gave two indications:

(a) he would come to the South seeking refuge;

(b) he would be known by 'three sayings;

This mystical reference to the "three sayings" indicated those three "madnesses" about which Aurobindo himself had spoken (and they have already been referred to) in his letters to his wife, Mrinalini. Thus the clues fitted exactly and Iyengar identified Sri Aurobindo as the "Uttaryogi" whom he sought easily. It was this Iyengar who published at his own cost the little Yogic book entitled "Yogic Sadhana" which Sri Aurobindo had "received" while experimenting with automatic writing. Since he had not really written the book himself, he later stopped its circulation.

Initial Troubles In Pondicherry

The early years in Pondicherry presented great difficulties before Aurobindo and his young companions.

First of all they had to suffer acute penury as there was practically no money or very little money. After all, there was no source either. They had to live in a small room almost denuded of any furniture. While others slept on the floor a thin bedding was, some how, arranged for Aurobindo. They had to practically starve as it was difficult for his friends to send him financial help and not to reveal his destination. It was quite dangerous in those days for anyone to help a revolutionary leader. Moreover, the British Police and the C.I.D had not yet given up Sri Aurobindo's chase. Even for years together he was kept under watch and frequently pestered by the government sleuths.

It was very difficult - as it would appear to any other institution steeped in the imperialistic values— to believe for the British Raj that Aurobindo's sole intention of going to Pondicherry was to practice yoga.

They thought that yoga and religion were mere tricks and facades to cover the revolutionary activities. All that they really believed in was the fact that "Aurobindo was most dangerous man in all India" - the one source of all their troubles and the master mind behind the entire "so-called" national struggle. Hence, their "logical deductions" were that revolutionary instructions and plans, - perhaps even bombs and pistols, were being supplied by him from his safe haven in Pondicherry and so it was that secret police agents constantly haunted his house, kept watch on every movement and made all attempts to do away with him. This opinion gave rise to many conspiratorial theories woven around Sri Aurobindo. The three of them are being mentioned below:

Conspiracy No.1

Such was the terror that the British government felt with Aurobindo "let loose" that it had placed police and its strength everywhere: even in Madras, on to the road to Pondicherry and indeed the town of Pondicherry as well. Pondicherry in those days was full of local 'goondas' too, and especially during the political election campaign anarchy was witnessed almost all over the town. It was during such a campaign that the British tried one of their worst moves.

The spies conspired with a local political leader who was influential and had some of these 'goondas' in his pay to carry off Aurobindo from the limits of French India, so that he could be immediately arrested by the British on some trumped-up charge. But as the good-luck would have it, Sri Aurobindo's young comrades-in-arms got hint of this plan, and arming themselves with acid bottles sat up the whole night to "welcome" the kidnappers!

But—nobody came! What had stopped them? Most strangely, on that very day, against this very leader, a warrant of arrest had been issued by the opposite political party, and it was he who had to run away from Pondicherry to Madras! Don't, dear readers, you suspect a hand of Providence in this marvellous 'poetic justice' which made the conspirators trapped in the game they laid for trapping Aurobindo?

Conspiracy No.2

Although having failed in its first attempt the British Police was not to give up its effort to trap Aurobindo and take him out of French India. The sleuths couldn't rest in peace for everyday more and more revolutionaries were crossing over French India as refugees. Looking to this situation the C.I.D tried another plan: they forged documents, collected photographs and maps and charts and some letters, packed them in a tin and secretly threw them into a well in the house of one of the revolutionaries, Aiyer, a good friend of Sri Aurobindo. The intention was to implicate the whole group and show that all of them were engaged in dangerous activities. However, as these British agents could not act openly in French territory, they engaged a local man, one Mayuresan, to inform the French police that if the house of these revolutionaries were searched, proofs of their conspiracies would be surely found. Once again Providence seemed to have interfered. The maid servant at Aiyar's place, drawing water from the well, happened to draw out the tin as well. On Sri Aurobindo's advice, the French police were immediately informed. They came and found in the tin seditious pamphlets and papers, some with image of Kali Goddess, some written in Bengali. The idea was to show that these refugees were carrying on secret correspondence with revolutionaries abroad and conspiring against the British government. As all houses were to be searched, the investing French Magistrate came to Aurobindo's room also. The room was almost bare a few trunks, a table and a chair. When he searched the table drawers and took out the papers, he was amazed to find even Latin and Greek on certain papers. The Magistrate was so surprised to find a Greek and Latin scholar at such a remote place in South India that he couldn't help expressing: "He knows Greek!

He knows Latin!" He was so impressed with the scholar yogi that he removed his men and went away, bowing his head to Aurobindo. The informer, Mayuresan, strongly threatened for making a false complaint, had to go but to quietly disappear from Pondicherry.

At this juncture, it should be mentioned that the French government - perhaps due to the traditional rivalry between the British and the French - had been quiet good to all those political refugees, shielding them as a point of honour. However, the British government was still game to get rid of the revolutionaries, and started putting much pressure on the French authorities to deport these revolutionaries or to hand them over to it. Even a proposal was made them to send them to Algiers - another French territory. Sri Aurobindo's friends, the Tamil Nationalist Leaders including among whom was also the poet-patriot Bharati, came to him in much excitement to ask whether he would prefer to leave India. Aurobindo remained silent for a couple of minutes and quietly and firmly replied: "Mr. Bharati, I am not going to budge an inch from here!" Others also accepted this discussion whole-heartedly and enthusiastically, and the idea was finally dropped.

Conspiracy No. 3

Although having failed twice in its attempt to implicate Aurobindo, the British Government did not give up looking for proofs, making false reports, gathering imaginary 'seditious' stories. One day Aurobindo and his young companions were utterly stunned by a most unforeseen event. Bijoy Nag, who accompanied Aurobindo to

Pondicherry, had a cousin suffering from TB. On the medical advice he came to Pondicherry, for a change of air, also hoping that Sri Aurobindo would cure him by his yogic power. With him had also come a companion and servant, Biren Roy, who, being a Bengali, soon became the general manager, cook etc. of Aurobindo's house. He became soon an almost indispensable member of that household.

Suddenly one day Biren had his head completely shaved. And seeing him, Moni, though usually very fashionable and particularly about his looks, also took a fancy for a complete head shave. Biren tried to persuade him to give up the idea but Moni was insistent and obstinate. A day or two later, late in the evening at about 10'clock, all the inmates were sitting around Sri Aurobindo, when there occurred something rather extraordinary. Biren suddenly stood up and shouted: "Do you know who I am? I am a spy, a C.I.D man! I can't keep it to myself any longer— I must speak out — I must confess — !" With these words he fell at Sri Aurobindo feet. Every one was dumbfounded. Could this be really true? Or a practical joke? They started laughing. But Biren thought they knew everything and were fooling him. He jumped up, went to the next room and brought Rs. 50/- (a big amount then) from his trunk. "See, here is the proof. Where could I have got all this money? This is the reward of my evil deed— spying on Sri Aurobindo! Never, never will I do this work again. I give you my word, I ask your forgiveness—." All sat silent and still. They did not know what to think and say.

This is how the third conspiratorial attempt was exposed prematurely. Biren had shaved his head so that the police spies might spot him as their man from rest of the young Bengalis. But, inadvertently, Moni, too, had his head shaved, leading Biren to suspect as though he, or perhaps all of them, had found out his secret and hence Moni shaving off his head rather deliberately! So partly out of fear of the exposure and partly out of true repentance but really due to his conscience pricking him that he confessed.

This incident made the atmosphere in the house quite serious and disturbed. All were worried. How could this have happened? A spy living in their very midst?! Bijoy was so furious that he would have done something drastic. However, fearing the revolutionaries retribution, Biren left and fled to as far away as Mesopotamia. Even after his departure tension was quite perceptible in the house. Trust appeared to have been the first casualty; suspicion walked through the roads. A large number of secret police agents still lurked in the town. Biren's confession again hinted at all this happening as though a part of the divine scheme. Aurobindo, all this while remained quiet and unperturbed. He had complete faith in his Divine Guide who could commit no faux pas in His planning for himself. He continued, non-challantly, performing his yogic meditation as though nothing had happened.

14

Arrival Of The Mother

We have already referred about a French woman called, Mira, who had reportedly developed a telepathic communion with Sri Aurobindo through the power of yoga. But it was March 29, 1914, at 3.30 p.m. that woman called the Mother, met Aurobindo for the first time. But going by her spiritual experience she claimed to have met him many years ago. Now for having direct 'Darshan' that she had come all the way from France to work with him. In an answer to a question, she explained her mission on earth in the following manner: "Between eleven and thirteen a series of psychic and spiritual experience revealed to me not only the existence of God but the possibility for meeting with Him or revealing Him integrally in consciousness and action, of manifesting Him upon earth in a life divine. This, along with practical discipline of its fulfillment, was given to me, during my body's sleep, by several teachers some of whom I met afterwards on the physical plane. Later on, as an interior and exterior development proceeded, the spiritual and psychic relation with one of those being became more and more clear— I was led to call Him Krishna and henceforth I was aware that it was with him (whom I should meet on earth one day) that the divine work had to be done—."

"The moment I saw Aurobindo I recognized him as the being I used to call Krishna— this is enough to explain why I am fully convinced that my place and work are near him in India."

Following this first meeting with Sri Aurobindo on March 30, Mother mentioned in her 'Meditations' the following thought:

"It matters not if there are hundred of beings plunged in the deepest ignorance. He whom we saw yesterday is here on earth. His presence is enough to prove that a day shall come when darkness shall be transformed into Light; When Thy reign shall indeed be established upon earth."

It was about this time, Paul Richard, a French thinker and scholar persuaded Sri Aurobindo to start a philosophical journal to give the world his vision and knowledge in terms of the intellect.

Só, "The Arya, A philosophical Review", was started on Sri Aurobindo's birthday, i.e. August 15, 1914. At that time he had completed his 42nd birthday. Between 1914 to 1920, in one vast sweep non-stop, Sri Aurobindo wrote prolifically. He wrote almost whole of his work: nearly five thousand pages, and most strangely, not one book after another, but four, five or even six books serialized at a time!

However, a few months later, World War I broke out and Richard was called back to France. With the result, Sri Aurobindo was left alone to write 64 pages of philosophy every month! But quietly, undisturbed he kept on writing. When asked how he could manage it he replied: "it is out of a silent mind that I write what ever comes ready-shaped from above." Sri Aurobindo's this explanation might appear baffling to many but the fact is that he appeared to have totally empathy with the Divine Voice. Although yoga means this sort of communion with Lord almighty, it is very rarely achievable. But there have been instances in India's spiritual history which assert that it is entirely and humanly possible. That Sri Aurobindo has achieved this rare communion is clear by his work. So outstanding yet equally copious. What ten authors might write in ten years was written, almost effortlessly, by him in a span of five years.

It was during this period that barring his 'Savitri', the 'Magnum opus', an epic were first written for the Arya. Many of these embodied the inner knowledge that had come to him in his practice of yoga; others were concerned with the spirit and significance of Indian civilization and culture, the true meaning of the Vedas. They represented the true meaning of the progress of human society; the nature of evolution of poetry; the possibility of the unification of the human races. They are still available in print under the following titles: *The Life Divine, The Synthesis of Yoga, The Human Cycle, The Ideal of Human Unity, Essays on the Gita, The Future Poetry, The Secret of the Veda, The Foundation of Indian Culture, The Isha-Upanishad.*

On February 21, 1915, the Mother's birthday was celebrated for the first time in Pondicherry. On Feb 22, the Mother wrote several letters which describe their common mission, their spiritual experiences, the trials they were facing in their unshakable faith in the ultimate victory.

For the readers must have observed quite drastic changes in Sri Aurobindo's life. It is apparently difficult to digest one man playing so many roles in one life span. He who was destined to be an English man and trained for this role; suddenly left the ICS deliberately even though it was cleared. Then he serves a Maharaja and shows his administrative acumen. But during this period he also develops the spirit of an armed revolutionary and finally leaving everything else, settles in Pondicherry to meditate, as commanded by the Divine voice and devotes his time to ameliorate the sufferings of humanity through his writings. It may be noticed that all of these roles are apparently poles apart. But he showed his class in everyone of them which clearly proves Sri Aurobindo to have been an especial creation of Lord Almighty.

By this time Sri Aurobindo was a person almost withdrawn from the world and totally devoted to his Sadhana.

15

Sadhana And Creative Work

It was on April 24, 1920 that the Mother returned to Pondicherry to stay there permanently. She had now come to join Sri Aurobindo in his work and Sadhana. Since then she never left Pondicherry again. With the arrival of the Mother, Aurobindo's 'Sadhana' became extremely intense and deep, particularly between 1920 to 1926. It was during his Sadhana that Aurobindo saw the magnitude of the spiritual work set before him that needed the concentration of all his energies. Years of inner striving and intense yoga were required for him to find a real way and trace it out completely. "But", as he had himself admitted: "the Sadhana and the work were waiting for the Mother's coming."

Thus far Sri Aurobindo had accepted no discipline. He lived in retirement with a few companions of his political days, with whom he had the relation of friends, not of the Guru and disciples. However, later on, there was a gradual development of spiritual relations and when the Mother came back, more people began to come to follow the spiritual path. It was thus that a community of Sadhaks (aspirants) was formed for the maintenance and guidance of those who had left everything behind for the sake of a higher life. Perhaps he could devote the whole time to his Sadhana because the Mother gradually took charge of the whole management of his household. It was her job to decide whatever arrangements had to be made for lodging, for the services of food, for decent living and hygiene. All these activities grew of themselves as the need arose, and slowly led to the foundation of the Ashram in Nov. 1926.

The Establishment of the Ashram

The beginning of 1926 witnessed the work of guiding disciples beginning to move exclusively towards the Mother. It was apparent that Aurobindo was slowly withdrawing to seclusion. It was the Mother who took up the great work: both of inner sadhana and of outer organization. Sri Aurobindo's daily meditation became more and more concentrated and intense. However, there was a strange feeling as if something of great significance was about to happen. A feeling grew in all the disciples that some higher power would descend. Sri Aurobindo himself had been working intensively and for a long time, perhaps preparing for this descend. At last on Nov. 24, 1926, the High Power descended. The Mother called this day 'the Day of Victory', for this descent marked a great step in Sri Aurobindo's life. Aurobindo himself called this power the "Over mind". He speaks of a still higher power, the "Supermind" which he also wanted to bring and brought down, on earth. Aurobindo himself explains these powers in the following manner: "By the Supermind is meant the full Truth - Consciousness of the Divine — Between the Supermind and the human mind there are a number of ranges, planes — The Overmind is the highest of these ranges; it is full of lights and powers—" He said, "The Overmind has to be reached and brought down before the Supermind descent is at all possible — for the Overmind is the passage—". Perhaps these explanations are too terse to be grasped by a normal mind, for the range of the ordinary mind is very limited. However, the same concept is again referred to by Sri Aurobindo in his famous epic - poem: "Savitri". Of this higher power, Sri Aurobindo says in his poem:

"There is a consciousness mind cannot touch,
Its speech cannot utter nor its thoughts reveal."

Nevertheless, it was on this day the most significant phase in Sri Aurobindo's mighty spiritual work began. On this very day he retired into complete solitude. As also, it was on this day "Sri Aurobindo Ashram" officially came into being under the overall care and guidance of the Mother. Although he had retired yet he didn't close his eyes. He still kept a close watch on all that was transpiring in the world. Not only this he also actively intervened whenever he thought his intervention was indispensable. He shared, too, the Mother's work of guiding the disciples mainly by writing letters, packed with inner help and power, explaining their difficulties, their experiences, directing them, giving them knowledge. In one of the letters answering a disciple's complaint for delay, he says: "You do not realize that I have to spend 12 hours over ordinary correspondence, numerous reports etc. I work three hours in the afternoon and whole night upto 6 in the morning over this."

In fact his letters - hundreds of which have been published by the Ashram reveal the clarity of thought and his pithy sayings. Some of them are being quoted, culled from his these letters, below:

The Gems of Thought: [Explaining the different shades of the meaning as conveyed by the words which are mistakenly often quoted as synonyms, he says:]

"Faith is a feeling in the whole being; belief is mental; confidence means trust in a person or in the Divine or a feeling of surety about the result of one's seeking or endeavour—"

And in another he guides to one in difficulty and reveals a sure method of knowing what is good for us:

"In moments of trial, faith in the divine protection and the call for protection; at all times the faith that what the Divine wills is the best." "It is what turns you toward the Divine that must be accepted as good for you —all is bad for you that turns you away from the Divine."

"Prayer should be full of confidence, without sorrow or lamenting."

****

"A sincere heart is worth all the extraordinary powers in the world."

[A simple direction for our inner progress and character building:]

To be able to be regular is great force, one becomes master of one's time and one's movements."

"Only those who sympathize can help-surely also one should be able to see the faults of others without hatred. Hatred injures both parties; it helps none."

"Sacrifice depends on the inner attitude. If one has nothing outward to sacrifice, one has always one self to give."

****

Perhaps Sri Aurobindo's general demeanour and his personality give the impression as though he had so sense of humour or that he was totally a dry person. This is not correct for he was a great humourist. Talking about sense of humour he said: "Sense of humour? It is the salt of existence. Without it the world would have gone utterly out of balance - it is unbalanced enough already— and rushed to blazes long ago."

****

His one of the pithiest directions to humanity is epitomized in the sentences quoted below:

"Remain firm through the darkness; the light is there and will conquer".

Even after retirement, Sri Aurobindo gave 'Darshan' in public four times a year. When asked, however why he had retired from outer activity, he said he had to keep himself out from the type of work which Mother was doing in order to find time for his 'real work'. Now let us learn about it as well.

16

His Work: Yoga And Poetry

Sri Aurobindo's contribution to the discipline of yoga has been tremendous. 'Yoga' is an ancient Indian discipline, believed to have been originated by Patanjali and it is vividly described in various Puranas as well. Literally 'yoga' means union. But 'union' with what or between which two entities? There are many interpretations. Some call it union between the mind and the body, some define it as the union of the human soul with the Divine; the union of man and God etc. All the paths, the ways and practices which lead to this union are called the path of yoga. But Sri Aurobindo's interpretation is: "It is the object of my yoga to transform life by bringing down into it the Light, Power and Bliss of the divine Truth—." He envisages that the final aim is to recreate a divine life on this earth and in the earthly existence. Sri Aurobindo, however, did not teach any escape from life on mere 'Sannyas'. He says: "we are here to do what the Divine wills and to create a world in which the Divine will can manifest its truth— Our yoga is not for our own sake but for the sake of Divine." Again, he expostulates on the objectives of the yoga discipline by saying: "The object of the yoga is to love the Divine for the Divine's sake alone, to be turned in our nature into the nature of the Divine, and in our will and works and life to be the instrument of the Divine:"

In a conclusive vein he sums up: "Its object is not to be a great yogi or a Superman——!"

However, this may raise a fresh query to many as to what or who is the Divine?

Sri Aurobindo, like all the ancient sages of India, tells us that behind the appearances of the Universe there is a Reality; a self of all things, one and eternal. This is "the Divine". All beings are united in that one self and spirit but are ignorant of their true Self and Reality because of a veil of separation in their nature. By yoga this "veil can be removed and man can become aware of his true Self; the Divinity within us and all things."

Sri Aurobindo's Concept of The Evolution

He teaches us that our world is the scene of an ascending evolution, which goes from the stone to plant, from plant to animal and from animal to man. Man, as it is generally believed, is the crown jewel of the creations of the Almighty and the very summit of His creative power. So, Aurobindo also believes that there is nothing on earth superior to him. He further warns man that he may be surely mistaken in this belief for, he believes, in his physical nature man is still wholly an animal, albeit a thinking and speaking one, yet an animal in habits and instincts still. So Sri

Aurobindo exhorts all that the next step of evolution ought to be taken: the animal man must become the divine man and for this he must develop a new higher spiritual consciousness. This is what Sri Aurobindo calls the Supermind or the Supramental. Man must reach upto this Truth - consciousness, and live a new life, perfectly harmonious, good and beautiful, happy and fully conscious.

Writing about Aurobindo, says the Mother: "He gave all his time to establish in himself this consciousness— and to help those gathered around him to realize it."

So, his "real work" as Aurobindo claimed was 'to bring down this great power to transform the earth-life and to show other the path of a new divine life upon the earth'. It is to this path and to this life that the Mother calls all the brave little children of the world-- to Truth's final victory. This is the path, according to him, of the Integral Yoga: to realize the Divine, to approach him with love and devotion and Bhakti; to serve Him with one's works and to know Him—finally to surrender all our nature to Him that it may be transformed and made divine by the Light of Truth.

However, from November, 1938, Sri Aurobindo found it necessary to change the course of his work, for the looming world crisis (the II War) needed a deeper concentration all the time. He also realized that the main movement of the inner spiritual work needed an undisturbed and single pointed concentration.

This was the time when he waged an Inner war. For, from the seclusion and solitude of his room he was waging a terrible spiritual battle with the forces of Darkness, the dark Satanic forces which oppose the coming of the Truth-Light. He had plunged deep, into the darkest Abyss of unconsciousness and false hood, into the utter Night, the storm and chaos of tumult, he had to fight a grim fierce battle before the Truth could be completely established here and the earth uplifted out of his darkness toward the divine.

In fact all his work was undertaken to bring Light and Truth and Peace and Joy to earth and humanity. He has himself proclaimed through — one of his numerous poems:

"In me the spirit of immortal love

Sketches its arms out to embrace mankind".

Perhaps it was because of his deep love for men that he took upon himself this terrible burden. Some might think that he was rather self-proclaimedly arrogating himself to attaining this alleged burden of entire humanity but the fact is that it is the question of one's inner sensitivity to perceive oneself as the representative of entire human race. It is the essence of the perception for the theory of incarnation in the Hindu thought. Lord Ram also saw the iniquity suffered by the holymen when he was around in the world. For the demons, the sin-perpetrations had not damaged his person in the least. But Ram also saw himself as the sole custodian of all that was righteous in the world. And hence his declaration upon seeing the heaps of the bones of those holymen and saints that were reportedly consumed by the demons: "Nishichar heen karon mahee;

Bhuj uthaya prana keen "[as mentioned in Tulsidas's 'Sri Ramcharita manas and meaning. 'I shall wipe out the demon race]."

Sri Aurobindo himself says: "It is only divine love which can bear the burden I have to bear, that all have to bear who have sacrificed everything else to the one aim of uplifting earth out of this darkness towards the divine."

In his one very beautiful poem, entitled 'Abyss', Sri Aurobindo speaks thus:

"I have been digging deep and long
Mid a horror of filth and mire
A bed for the golden river's song
A home for the deathless fire!"

That this battle is endless one is clear by his assertion:

"My gaping wounds are a thousand and one"!

He says and again;

"I have laboured and suffered the Matter's night
To bring the fire to man".

But not only do the dark forces struggle against the Truth, the whole earth resists and man himself:

"The Truth and Truths men fear and deny,
The light of lights they refuse——"

And so, "each battle has to be fought and re-fought," he says. But not only did Sri Aurobindo wage his spiritual war secretly, he also used his force in a constant action upon the world forces. When, for instance, during the II War he saw behind Hitler and Nazism there were dark Asuric forces, and that they were victorious all mankind would be enslaved to the tyranny of evil and the spiritual evolution of man suffer a set back, "he actively intervened, just at the critical moment of Dunkirk, and the whole tide of war turned in the favour of the Allies." Although it is claimed by his staunch admirers it is too simplistic explanation to offer to explain the expiry of the most complicated confrontation in human history. However, his spiritual contribution to maintaining a rigid model of righteousness cannot be denied. So, too, it is claimed that he intervened with his spiritual forces against the Japanese aggression when it became evident that Japan intended to attack and invade and conquer India. And "once again the tide of Japanese victory changed immediately into a rapid defeat" when the Allied Forces dropped a nuclear bomb upon Japan. Though this change may be again attributed to his spiritual forces, yet invisibly there had been many peace lovers who wanted it to happen this way, and whose spiritual contribution can't be gainsaid either.

India's Independence

There is no doubt that in India's independence struggle Sri Aurobindo's contribution was truly great. Not only through his revolutionary activity but also through his writings and exhortations he managed to surge forth a wave which continued to billow till India achieved its independence. In this case the spiritual power which many yogis hold is greater than any other force and more effective did show its miracle rather invisibly. Nearly half a century long efforts of him did see their culmination in India eventually attaining its freedom on August 15, 1947. It was this power that Sri Aurobindo put into the movement of India's liberation that did show its effect. It was, as it is claimed by his admirers, and to a large extent rightly so, not a coincidence or a chance accident but "the sanction and seal of the Divine force" upon his work that India declared in self free on his birthday. The message he gave for this day is so heart-stirring, so charged with words of destiny that its gist is given below:

"August 15th, 1947 is the birthday of free India. It marks for her the end of an old era, the beginning of a new age. But we can also make it by our life and acts as a free nation an important date in a new age opening for the whole world, for the political, social, cultural and spiritual future of humanity.

"August 15th is my own birthday and it is naturally gratifying to me that it should have assumed this vast significance— Indeed on this day I can watch almost all the world movements which I had hoped to see fulfilled in my life time, though they then looked like impracticable dreams arriving at fruition or on their way to achievement. In all these movements free India may well play a large part and take a leading position.

"The first of these dreams was a revolutionary movement which would create a free united India. India today is free but it has not achieved unity— The old communal divisions into Hindus and Muslims seems now have hardened into a political division of the country[1]. —If it lasts India may be seriously weakened, even crippled; civil strife may always remain possible even with a new invasion and foreign conquest. India's internal development and prosperity may be impeded — her destiny impaired — This must not be; the partition must go; unity must and will be achieved, for it is necessary for the greatness of India's future.

"Another dream was for the resurgence and liberation of the people of Asia and her return to her great role in the progress of human civilization —. There India had her part to play and has begun to play it with an energy and ability which already indicate the measure of her possibilities and the place she can take in the council of nations.

"The third dream was a world- union forming the outer basis of a fairer, brighter and nobler life for all mankind —that unification of the human world is under way — Here too, India has begun to play a prominent role — A new spirit of oneness will take hold of the human race.

"Another dream, the spiritual gift of India to the world has already begun —. Amid the disasters of the time more and more eyes are turning towards her with hope and there

---

1. Sri Aurobindo is referring here to the division of India into "India" and "Pakistan".

is even an increasing resort not only to her teachings, but to her psyche and spiritual practice.

"The final dream was a step in evolution which would raise man to a higher and larger consciousness —. This evolution — since it must proceed through a growth of the spirit — the initiative can come from India and — the central movement may be hers:

"Such is the content which I put into this day of India's liberation—."

Don't we catch the old refrain from the Gita mouthed by Lord Krishna:

"I am raising up this nation to send forth my word— it is for the world— that they arise— I am giving them freedom for the service of the world."

Sri Aurobindo's Poetic Creations

Although we have discussed Sri Aurobindo' political and spiritual thoughts and generally know him as a great thinking saintly figure that bestow the Indian firmament with his radiant concepts, he was essentially a poet. Poetry is generally believed to be the essence of thoughts in reflection, shouldered by metaphors and similes and it is truly applicable on Sri Aurobindo. In fact while his thoughts were conveyed to public through his writings, their concise and crystallized form was converted into his poetry. Although this trait of his was been occasionally hinted at only in passing, he had been writing poetry from his days in England and then in Baroda as well. It was during the final years of his stay in

Pondicherry that he started devoting more time to it. His early lyrical poetry is very beautiful and wonderful; with touches of deep insight everywhere. During his Baroda period he composed his long narrative poems "Love And Death" and "Urvasie". The culmination of this prowess resulted in his creating his magnum opus "Savitri". The conquest of Death by Love, the theme of this early poem, is on a different level while the theme of 'Savitri' though derived from this theme, hits you at a different level. The first draft of 'Savitri' was prepared during this period only. During his political period too, he wrote many, many poems and plays. Some of which were published in his political journey. In one of the plays written on Shivaji's period, there is the story of Baji Prabhou, the great hero, Shivaji's friend whose courage and noble self-sacrifice knew no bounds for he knew that man derives his all strength from the Divine.

But of course, Sri Aurobindo's finest poetical work belongs to the Pondicherry period. He says of his philosophical writings: "Everything I wrote came from yogic experience, knowledge and inspiration." He further writes: "So too my greater power over poetry and perfect expression was acquired — from the heightening of my consciousness."

The most lovely lyrics, the most powerful sonnets, the miraculous hexameter epic "ILION", narrative poems and lyrics in quantitative and new meters, all are crowded into this period. They are the poems conveying deep spiritual experience. His poetry is essentially a poetry of the soul and not, as generally believed about poetry, poetry of heart. Even in the most emotional contexts, the reason guided by the voice of the inner conscience or soul. Even in his magnum opus 'Savitri' this may be found present in abundance. 'Savitri' is actively a story from Indian mythology. The whole poem is developed as an allegory. While Savitri represents Love, and Yamaraj represents Death. The brief story is given below. Once you know it well the few poetic nuances or allegorical similes and metaphor may give their true meaning.

The Story of Savitri

There was a king, Aswa-pati, who had no child, and for eighteen years he prayed to Savitri, wife of Brahma, asking that he might have a child to continue his name. When at last the goddess appeared to him from the midst of his sacrificial fire, she told him she was very pleased with his devotions and would grant him a boon. He asked that he might have sons to honour him. The goddess, however, said she had spoken with Brahma about this, and it was not possible, but he would have a daughter who would be radiantly beautiful.

`The king accepted the gift with pleasure, and in a short time he became the father of a beautiful girl who, when she grew up, was indeed so beautiful that people called her a daughter of the gods. And perhaps because of her very beauty no one asked her to marry him. Her father then sent her on a visit to the surrounding countries. She travelled in a golden car, followed by well-tried servants, and in the charge of good counsellors. She visited many countries and finally made her way home again. When she arrived the sage Narada was with her father, and when he saw her he asked the king why she was not married. Aswapati told him of her journey and said he could stay and listen to her story if he wished.

Savitri told her father she had found the one of her choice. In the forest she had seen Satyavan, son of Dyumatsena, a blind king whose kingdom had been stolen from him and who was now living with his wife and son in the forest where they had spent years in austerities. The son had grown to be a man and she wished to marry him.

Her father turned to Narada and asked for particulars of the youth. Narada said he was brave, wise and good - in fact he had all the virtues-but the tragedy was he had only one more year to live. Hearing this, her father asked her if she would go again into the world and make another choice. But she was firm in her resolve to marry Satyavan so he gave the marriage his blessing. Narada then departed and went to heaver

Preparations were made for the journey to the forest, and father and daughter set out with many gifts for Satyavan's father. When they arrived they were greeted warmly, the gifts were given, and the reason of their visit explained. Dyumatsena said he and his wife and son spent their lives in religious austerities and they could not expect the princess to share these hardships with them. But Aswapati told him that his daughter was determined and also he himself had always wanted an alliance with him. So in the end the marriage was arranged, neighbouring priests were sent for and, attired in her best and gorgeous clothes, Savitri became the wife of Satyavan. Then her father left and Savitri took off her royal garments, put on the hermit's dress of bark, and began her life of service to her husband and his parents. She was so dutiful, kind and helpful, that they loved her very much.

But time, inexorable, moved on until there remained only four days to the time when Satyavan would die. All through this period Savitri had thought of his approaching death and wondered what could be done. She had fasted for days and nights, and now she decided to fast and stand up for three days and three nights without rest. Though the king told her it was too arduous a task for her to perform she insisted, and at the end of the period she was very weak. She spent the last night before the fateful day sorrowing and wondering what she could do.

In the morning she got up and did the usual work of the day and the usual devotional exercises, and then went to her parents-in-law. The king told her that now her vow was completed she should eat, but she put the request aside and said she would eat at nightfall. She asked if they would give her permission to go to the forest with her husband that day, for she had not been before and she would like to go. The king eagerly granted this request — the first she had made. Satyavan tried to prevent her, for he said the way was rough, but her mind was made up and they both set out to the woods where Satyavan used to gather fruit and cut down wood for their fires. As they went in the forest she saw gaily coloured peacocks, little streams, and masses of beautiful flowers, and her heart grew even more devoted to Satyavan as he pointed out the beauties they were passing. But the sorrow of the fateful moment hung heavy on her mind.

When they had obtained all the fruit that was necessary Satyavan started to cut the wood.

After a while he stopped and said his head was aching and his limbs did not seem strong enough to support him, so he would lie down and sleep for a bit. Savitri placed his head on her lap, and thought of Narada's words. Then she saw the awful but majestic figure of the god Yama, with the noose of death. Quickly she laid down her husband's head and stood up to face him and asked who he was. He told her he was Yama, and as her husband's life was finished he had come to take him away. She asked why he himself had come, for it was his messengers who sought out the dying, not he himself. Yama said that was true, but Satyavan was a virtuous and noble soul, and therefore it was not fitting that only the messengers of death came for him. As he was speaking he drew out Satyavan's soul, no bigger than a thumb, bound it fast in his noose and began to leave the lifeless body on the ground.

Then the determination and devotion of Savitri were stirred to their utmost and she followed him. Yama told her she should not come for it was her duty to prepare the funeral rites for her husband, but she answered it was her duty to go wherever her husband went, and that as she had performed all the domestic rites which were considered the most important, she would follow him. Yama was pleased with this answer and asked her what boon she would like. He said he would give her anything she wanted except the life of her husband.

She asked that the blind king should have his sight restored and regain his former majesty. Yama granted this. Then he told her the journey was difficult and she must turn back. Savitri, however, said she could not be weary if she was with her husband, and she would go wherever he went, for the company of the good was always desirable.

Yama, pleased with these words, granted her another boon - anything save the life of her husband. This time she asked that the king should regain his kingdom and never lose it again.

Yama granted this, and again asked her to turn back, but with carefully guarded speech, she pleased him, and he granted her another boon.

This time she asked that her own father, who has no children but herself, should have one hundred sons.

Yama promised this too, but said she really must turn back as already she had come much further than she ought to have done. But she would not.

She asked another boon, that she should have one hundred sons and that was granted.

But even the gods get weary of constant questioning, and Yama granted her one last boon, the greatest of all. This time, then Savitri said, it must be a free boon, and he agreed. So she asked for the life of her husband for, she said, without him her life was impossible, and as Yama had already granted her one hundred sons, how could he take away her husband! She begged that he would let Satyavan live and at last Yama gracefully gave in.

This epic 'Savitri' containing over 23,800 lines, is known as Sri Aurobindo's magnum opus. He wrote and re-wrote through the years, polished and perfected to embody his vast vision of Truth; his spiritual vision of the universe and of life his vision of the future when the world would "manifest the unveiled Divine." His all spiritual knowledge, his command over the language, his entire intimate knowledge and experience of all the places of existence, from the darkest depths to the supreme heights, the shining words of Truth are all part of this wonderful epic. In his poem Aurobindo tells of Savitri, "the Divine word, daughter of Sun[1] / Goddess of the supreme Truth who comes down to save Satyavan." Using the entire tale as an allegory, Sri Aurobindo describes Satyavan soul's capture by Death God, Yama, as: "the soul — descended into the grip of death and ignorance." It is so that Savitri, the incarnation of the Divine Mother in Sri Aurobindo's poem, asks of the Lord this final boon:

"Thy embrace which rends the living knot of pain,

Thy joy, O Lord, in which all creatures breath,

Thy magic flowing waters of deep love

Thy sweetness give to me for earth and men."

And she is promised that when all her work is done, a new power will wake in man:

---

1. Also called 'Savitur' from which the word Savitri is derived. Savitri literally means of the Sun, the symbol of the Supermind or Truth-Consciousness.

"The Eternal's truth shall mould his thoughts and acts,
The Eternal's truth shall be his light and guide;
All then shall change, a magic order come —
A divine harmony shall be earth's law,
Beauty and Joy remould her way to live —
Nature shall live to manifest secret God —
This earthly life become the life divine."

These lines represent Sri Aurobindo's vision of future. The Mother says of 'Savitri: "Its revelation is prophetic."

"It is intuitive revealing poetry," and its language is "inspired, inevitable word,"

In fact Aurobindo had continued to revise and recast it in his lordly, leisurely way till the very end.

17

His End And The Ashram's Subsequent Activities

It was in Sept. 1950, that one day Aurobindo said to his disciple-scribe: "I must finish 'Savitri' soon." As we know he had been all through revising and perfecting his this epic work. But since he always worked unhurriedly and in a leisurely manner, his saying this kind of hurry created a sort of a stir in the Ashram. Why should he say so? Any premonition? However, it was only on December 5, 1950, that the real meaning behind his unusual hurry could be realized. Early hours on this day Aurobindo decided to leave his mortal coil. It was apparently 'Ichcha mrityu' as it is called in Indian etymology which literally means "dying at will." Like all great yogis he appeared to have mastered over death for he didn't suffer any difficulty at the last time and quitted his mortal coil without much ado. That it was a willed, deliberate withdrawl is what we all believe but the Mother confirmed it by saying: "Our Lord has sacrificed totally for us — He was not compelled to leave his body;

he chose to do so for reasons so sublime that they are beyond the reach of human mentality." Perhaps we have, in a way, his own 'explanation' in 'Savitri'!

"He must pass to the other shore of falsehood's sea,

He must enter the world's dark to bring there light —

He must enter the eternity of night

And know God's darkness as He knows his Sun,

For this he must go down into the pit.

For this he must invade the dolorous vasts —

Then shall be ended here the Law of Pain."

The Mother also said: "He has sacrificed his physical life in order to help more fully his work of transformation."

Following his physical end, his shining, majestic body lay in state - as thousands of people passed by having his last 'Darshan'- for more than four days. But it remained perfectly unchanged, for, as the Mother explained, it was charged with deep concentration of Supramental Light.

On 9th December, the body was laid in the vault prepared in the Centre of the Ashram courtyard. It seemed as though through and in his body this grand light had entered the very earth. As Aurobindo had said "Bringing the fires of the splendours of God into the human abyss."

The Mother wrote the beautiful thanksgiving and prayer which is engraved upon his Samadhi:

"To Thee who hast been the material envelope of our master, to Thee our infinite gratitude. Before Thee who hast done so much for us, who hast worked, struggled, suffered, hoped, endured so much, before Thee who has willed all, attempted all, prepared, achieved all for us, before Thee we bow down to implore that we may never forget, even for a moment, all we owe to Thee."

With this last magnificent self-giving, Sri Aurobindo seems to have achieved his purpose as he had described in his poem:

"The gulf twixt the depths and the heights is bridged

And the golden waters pour

Down the sapphire mountain rainbow-ridged

And glimmer from shore to shore

Heaven's fire's lit in the breast of the earth

And the undying sun's here burn——"

The Ashram Activities After Him

It goes to the credit of the Mother that Sri Aurobindo's work after him not only continued but grew even vaster and richer. The Ashram was founded with only 26 aspirants and now it has a vast multitude of them. There are people there of all types and 'traditions', of various nationalities of all ages and social classes. Aurobindo had once said: "It (Ashram) is a vast 'laboratory'", a field of experiment where all the basic difficulties of human nature, all the problems of human life are faced and conquered in conformity with what Sri Aurobindo had aspired: "To know the highest Truth and to be in harmony with it is the condition of right being, to express it in all that we are, experience and do is the condition of right living."

In 1951, "with the purpose of realizing one of Sri Aurobindo's most cherished ideals," the Mother founded the "Sri Aurobindo International Centre of Education". She declared that Sri Aurobindo had considered the formation of such a centre "as one of the best means of preparing future humanity to receive the Supramental light that will transform the elite of today into a new race manifesting upon earth the new light and force and life."

The centre follows Sri Aurobindo's principles of teaching and works on the lines laid down by the Mother.

AUROVILLE

Years ago the Mother had foreseen a model township, a symbol of human unity and world brother -hood. So a new city called 'AUROVILLE'- the city of Dawn- The city of Aurobindo was established on Feb. 28, 1968 with the Mother herself inaugurating it. In its foundation urn is mixed the soil of about a hundred and twenty countries of the world and the soil of Sri Aurobindo Ashram and the soil of Auroville. This acts as a beacon radiating Sri Aurobindo's power and world-vision. Now all the world over Centres have been started for teaching and practice of Sri Aurobindo's yoga, spreading the light which came into being way back in a small town of the then Bengal to enlighten the world, and which said:

"I saw the Omnipotent's flaming pioneers
Over the heavenly verge which turns towards life
Come crowding down the amber stairs of birth;
Forerunners of divine multitude
Out of the paths of the morning star they came —
I saw them cross the twilight of an age,
The sun-eyed children of marvellous dawn —
The architects of immorality."

The Prayer (Created by the Mother)

The following prayer is said everyday at Auroville

"MAKE OF US THE HERO WARRIORS
WE ASPIRE TO BECOME
MAY WE FIGHT SUCCESSFULLY
THE GREAT BATTLE OF THE FUTURE THAT IS BORN
AGAINST THE PAST THAT SEEKS TO ENDURE;
SO THAT THE NEW THINGS MAY MANIFEST
AND WE BE READY TO RECEIVE THEM".

****

Sri Aurobindo / 128

"Learn for thy soul's support on Heaven's strength
Turn towards high Truth, aspire to love and peace—".

Aurobindo